American Lives

Meriwether Lewis

Elizabeth Raum

Heinemann Library
Chicago, Illinois

© 2004 Heinemann Library
a division of Reed Elsevier Inc.
Chicago, Illinois

Customer Service 888-454-2279

Visit our website at www.heinemannlibrary.com

Designed by Sarah Figlio
Photo research by Alan Gottlieb
Printed in China

08 07 06 05
10 9 8 7 6 5 4 3

Library of Congress
Cataloging-in-Publication Data
Raum, Elizabeth.
  Meriwether Lewis / by Elizabeth Raum.
    v. cm. -- (American lives)
Includes bibliographical references (p.) and index.
Contents: Brave little hunter -- Child of the Revolution -- School days-- Planter and soldier -- President's secretary -- Planner -- Explorer -- Peace maker -- Grizzly bears and mountains -- Pacific Ocean -- Hero-- Governor -- Lewis's last days.
ISBN 1-4034-4193-6 -- ISBN 1-4034-4201-0 (pbk.)
1. Lewis, Meriwether, 1774-1809--Juvenile literature. 2.Explorers--West (U.S.)--Biography--Juvenile literature. 3. Lewis and Clark Expedition (1804-1806)--Juvenile literature. 4. West (U.S.)--Discovery and exploration--Juvenile literature. 5. West (U.S.)--Biography--Juvenile literature. [1. Lewis, Meriwether, 1774-1809. 2. Explorers. 3. West (U.S.)--Discovery and exploration.] I. Title. II. American lives (Heinemann Library (Firm)) F592.7.L42R38 2003
  917.804'2'092--dc21
                    2003004975

Acknowledgments
The author and publishers are grateful to the following for permission to reproduce copyright material: Title page, pp. 5, 11 Independence National Historical Park, Philadelphia; p. 4 Culver Pictures; pp. 7, 9, 23 Bettmann/Corbis; p. 8 North Wind Picture Archives; p. 10 Michael Haynes Historic Art; p. 12 Louis Archambualt, artist, Helena Montana, www.members.aol.com/injwif; p. 13 Library of Congress/Neg.#LC-USZC4-2970; p. 14 National Archives; p. 15 Hulton Archive/Getty Images; p. 16 Smithsonian American Art Museum/Washington, DC/Art Resource, NY; p. 17 National Museum of Wildlife Art, Jackson, Wyoming; p. 18T Oregon Historical Society, neg. #OrHi 101538; p. 18B Oregon Historical Society, neg. #OrHi 101540; pp. 19, 21 Gilcrease Museum; p. 20 Clymer Museum of Art; p. 22 Idaho State Historical Society, neg. # 2715; p. 24 Courtesy American Antiquarian Society; p. 25 American Philosophical Society; p. 26 Missouri Historical Society, St. Louis; p. 27 Missouri Historical Society, St. Louis, photograph by Cary Horton; p. 28 Burstein Collection/Corbis; p. 29 Bobby Mays/Corbis

Cover photograph by Independence National Historical Park, Philadelphia

The author thanks Sheldon Green, her friend and colleague at Concordia College, Moorhead, Minnesota, for sharing his expertise about the journeys of Lewis and Clark.

The publisher would like to thank Michelle Rimsa for her comments in the preparation of this book.

Every effort has been made to contact copyright holders of any material reproduced in this book. Any omissions will be rectified in subsequent printings if notice is given to the publisher.

Some words are shown in bold, **like this.** You can find out what they mean by looking in the glossary.

For more information on the image of Meriwether Lewis that appears on the cover of this book, turn to page 9.

Contents

Brave Little Hunter

When he was only eight years old, Meriwether would go hunting in the middle of the night. That was the best time to catch raccoons and opossums. Meriwether would take his guns and his dogs and head into the forest. Not even snow or cold could stop young Meriwether if he decided to do something. Everyone who knew him agreed that Meriwether was a brave boy.

Meriwether's skills as a young boy led to a lifetime of great adventures.

Years later, President Thomas Jefferson sent Meriwether on a journey across North America. On the journey, Meriwether met many Native American people. He wrote about animals and plants that were unknown to people in the eastern United States. The trip was filled with many dangers, but Meriwether bravely faced each problem.

Meriwether Lewis has been called "the greatest pathfinder this country has ever known."

Child of the Revolution

Meriwether Lewis was born on August 18, 1774, in Albemarle County, near Charlottesville, Virginia. His father, William Lewis, owned a large **plantation** called Locust Hill. As a boy, Meriwether watched **estate** workers growing vegetables, cutting trees, making cloth, and caring for farm animals.

There were few trained doctors in Virginia in the 1700s. Meriwether's mother, Lucy Meriwether Lewis, knew which plants and **herbs** made good medicine. She taught Meriwether how to use herbs to cure sickness.

Lucy Meriwether Lewis was a good mother to her son.

The Life of Meriwether Lewis

1774	1794	1801	1804
Born on August 18, in Albemarle County, Virginia	Became a soldier	Became President Jefferson's secretary	Left on **expedition**

The **Revolutionary War** began in 1775. On July 4, 1776, the United States **declared** its freedom from Britain. William Lewis, Meriwether's father, joined the army and was away for the next several years. When Meriwether was five years old, his father died in the war. The plantation went to Meriwether, the oldest son. But he was too young to manage a big plantation. His uncle ran it for him.

This is the cabin that now stands at Lewis's birthplace.

Thomas Jefferson

Thomas Jefferson was a neighbor and friend of the Lewis family when they lived in Virginia. Jefferson, who became the third president of the United States, knew and liked young Meriwether.

1805	1806	1807	1809
Reached the Pacific Ocean	*Returned to St. Louis in September*	*Appointed* **governor** *of Louisiana* **Territory**	*Died on October 11*

School Days

Meriwether's mother cared about books and education. She made sure that Meriwether attended school. At home, he learned good manners and how to dance. When Meriwether was eight or nine years old, his stepfather, Captain John Marks, moved the family to northeastern Georgia. It was in Georgia that Meriwether learned how to live in the wilderness. Once, when he was hunting with some friends, an angry bull rushed at them. While his friends looked on, Meriwether raised his gun and killed the bull. His bravery and quick thinking saved their lives.

Young boys only went to school for a few years before taking over chores and responsibilities at home.

When he was about thirteen, Meriwether returned to Virginia. He lived with his Uncle Nicholas, who had been taking care of Locust Hill. Now it was time for Meriwether to learn how to manage the **plantation.** Meriwether and his cousin, Peachy Gilmer, went to school together. They learned math, **botany,** and **geography.** Peachy later said that Meriwether was stubborn, quick to anger, and brave.

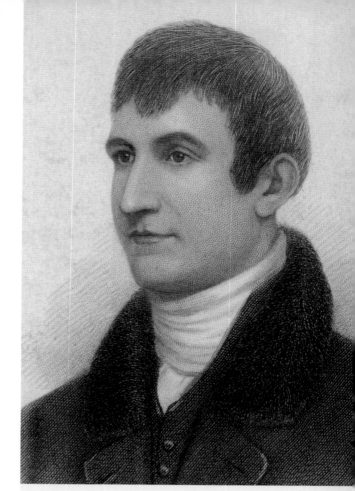

Meriwether experienced a lot of change in his young life. He often had to help take care of his family.

Four years later, when Meriwether's stepfather died, his mother decided to live with her family in Virginia. Seventeen-year-old Meriwether left school to help her move.

Planter and Soldier

Once he and his mother returned to Virginia, Meriwether took over running Locust Hill. He was good at managing the **plantation.** He grew tobacco and vegetables and raised farm animals. He enjoyed dancing and visiting with friends, but soon became bored with the daily work of running a large farm. Meriwether was pleased when his mother was able to take over.

Meriwether joined the U.S. Army in 1794 and served in a special rifle company.

William Clark was a captain in the U.S. Army. Meriwether was assigned to Clark's unit.

When President George Washington called for help to stop the **Whiskey Rebellion** in western Pennsylvania, twenty-year-old Meriwether volunteered. Army life pleased him. He liked travel, and he enjoyed being a leader. He began as a **private,** but was soon **promoted.** Eventually he became a captain. While Meriwether was in the army, he met William Clark, who later became his partner in exploring the West.

President's Secretary

Thomas Jefferson was elected president of the United States in 1801. Jefferson needed someone he could trust to be his secretary. He had heard that his young neighbor Meriwether Lewis was in the army. When the president asked Meriwether to be his secretary, Lewis agreed. As the president's secretary, Lewis gathered information for Thomas Jefferson, and he carried reports and messages to **Congress.** Lewis lived in the President's House.

President Jefferson and Lewis planned the expedition together at Monticello, Jefferson's home in Virginia.

The President's House

The home of the U.S. President has had several names, including the President's House, the President's Palace, and the Executive Mansion. President Theodore Roosevelt named it the White House in 1901.

Lewis studied with people from the University of Pennsylvania and gathered information about a possible route for the journey.

In the evenings, President Jefferson and Lewis talked about the future of the United States. Jefferson said that he wanted to send an explorer west across North America to map a trail from the Mississippi River to the Pacific Ocean. The president wanted to learn about the land and the plants and animals of the West. He also wanted information about the Native Americans who lived there. Lewis was eager to make the trip. Jefferson agreed that Lewis was the right man to lead an **expedition.**

Planner

Lewis and the president began planning for the **expedition.** They talked about how many people to take, what boats and supplies to bring, and what gifts to bring for the Native Americans. Jefferson asked Lewis to keep a journal and to treat Native Americans kindly. Lewis prepared for the trip by learning **botany** so he could describe plants, **astronomy** so he could find his way using the stars, and medicine so that he could help his people if they got sick.

Lewis's journals listed the gifts brought by the explorers for the Native Americans they met.

Louisiana Purchase

*On April 30, 1803, the United States purchased 828,000 square miles (more than a million square kilometers) of land from France. This was called the **Louisiana Purchase.** Lewis and Clark explored part of the Louisiana Purchase.*

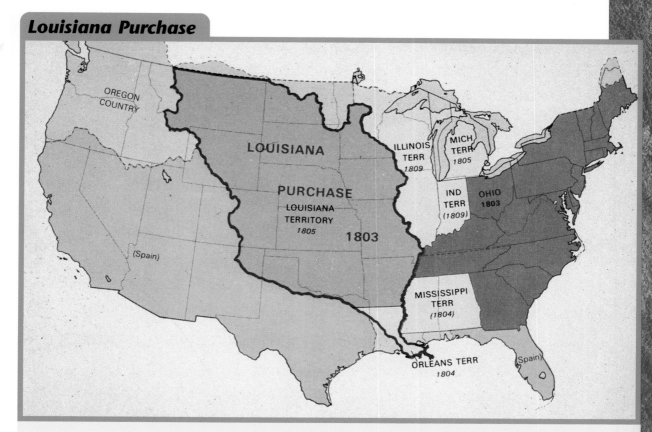

The purchase of the Louisiana Territory doubled the size of the United States. However, it needed to be explored to find out what was there and how far the territory actually went. Lewis and his men explored, scouted, **surveyed,** and mapped the lands of the Louisiana Purchase.

Lewis wrote to his army friend William Clark, asking him to help lead the expedition. Clark was a soldier and mapmaker. The two men trusted one another. Lewis promised Clark that they would both be captains and lead the expedition together. Clark agreed to go.

Explorer

Existing maps stopped at the Mandan villages near present-day Bismarck, North Dakota. Lewis would have to figure out the rest of the way to the Pacific Ocean. Lewis had little information about the people and places along the way. Fur traders told strange stories of woolly mammoths who roamed the prairies, giants who spoke strange languages, and mountains made of salt. Native Americans also gave them some information about what lay beyond. Lewis did not know what he would discover on the way west.

The Missouri River was shallow and muddy when Lewis used it to travel north on the **expedition.**

Seaman

Lewis bought a dog for the trip. Seaman was a black Newfoundland who was a good swimmer. He helped the expedition by hunting squirrels, geese, and beavers. Sometimes Seaman kept Lewis awake at night because he barked when he heard bears.

On May 21, 1804, Lewis and the explorers left St. Charles, Missouri. Travel on the Missouri River was dangerous, but they made good progress. They hunted deer, turkey, geese, and elk. They camped at the river's edge. They saw prairie dogs, coyotes, and pronghorn antelopes. These animals were unknown to scientists in the eastern part of the country.

Mosquitoes were a constant problem for the team. Mosquitoes were especially dangerous because they carried a disease called **malaria.** Many of the men, including Lewis, caught this disease.

Lewis liked prairie dogs so much that he shipped a live one to President Jefferson.

Peacemaker

Whenever Lewis met Native American chiefs, he gave a speech about peace and informed them about the **Louisiana Purchase.** He gave them peace medals as a gift from President Jefferson. Throughout the trip, Native Americans helped Lewis by giving him directions, food, shelter, horses, and boats. Without this help, the **expedition** would have failed.

Lewis often went wandering in the woods alone. He liked to be by himself and to look for new plants, animals, and birds.

Lewis gave peace medals like these to all the Native American chiefs he saw in Missouri.

Lewis brought many gifts for the Native Americans, including clothes, tobacco, paint, knives, and beads.

In October 1804, the Mandan welcomed Lewis to their villages. The Mandan villages were a major trading center. Lewis visited them to learn about the Mandan people.

At Fort Mandan, Lewis met Toussaint Charbonneau, a fur trader, and his Shoshoni wife, Sacagawea. The Charbonneaus asked to go west with him. Lewis agreed. He hired Charbonneau to act as an **interpreter.** Lewis hoped Sacagawea would ask the Shoshoni people to sell him some horses to carry men and supplies across the Rocky Mountains.

Grizzly Bears and Mountains

On April 7, 1805, the **expedition** left the Mandan villages. They saw huge herds of buffalo. Lewis and his men were chased by a grizzly bear. Lewis killed the bear, but it took several bullets.

One day in August, Lewis was wandering alone when he met some Shoshoni. They took him to their chief, Cameahwait, who was Sacagawea's brother. Cameahwait agreed to sell 29 horses to Lewis.

Lewis and his men ran into many wild animals during their trip. They had to fight to stay alive.

On May 26, 1805, Lewis saw the Rocky Mountains for the first time.

The trip across the Rocky Mountains was very difficult because of heavy snow. The men had no food and were so hungry that they had to kill and eat one of the horses. When they finally left the mountains, they met Native Americans who gave them food and shelter. Lewis became very ill after eating too much of the food. Lewis and the men rested until they were well enough to travel again.

Pacific Ocean

On the other side of the Rocky Mountains, the explorers found a beautiful valley and rivers full of fish. With the help of the **Nez Percé,** they built and sailed canoes down the Clearwater River to the Snake River and finally to the Columbia River. There were plenty of fish to eat, especially salmon, but the men soon got tired of fish. Lewis bought dogs from a local tribe and cooked them for his team.

The Nez Percé had never seen white men before the **expedition** arrived. According to tribal history, the Nez Percé had to decide between killing or being friendly to the strangers.

Since there were no maps to show the way, Lewis and Clark did not know how to get to the Pacific Ocean. Lewis went ahead with a small group of men. He reached the ocean on November 14, 1805. A few days later, when Clark and his group went out, they found Lewis's name carved in a tree near the shore. Clark added the date to the tree carving.

Lewis's abilities as a leader and explorer helped him successfully lead 40 men over land to the Pacific Ocean.

President Jefferson had hoped that Lewis could take a ship home. All winter Lewis searched the shore for ships, but none ever came. He and his team had to return over land.

Hero

On March 23, 1806, the **expedition** headed home. When Lewis and Clark arrived in St. Louis, Missouri, on September 23, 1806, people cheered and called them heroes. There were parties and parades. Lewis made his way to Locust Hill to see his mother. Then he traveled to Washington, D.C., to meet with President Jefferson. Lewis spent the winter in the President's House in Washington. People gave dinners in Lewis's honor, and he told them about his daring adventures.

This newspaper article announced the arrival of Lewis and his men in St. Louis.

By the last Mails.

MARYLAND. BALTIMORE, OCT. 29, 1806.

A LETTER from *St. Louis (Upper Louisiana)*, dated *Sept.* 23, 1806, announces the arrival of Captains LEWIS and CLARK, from their expedition into the interior.—They went to the *Pacific Ocean*; have brought some of the natives and curiosities of the countries through which they passed, and only lost one man. They left the *Pacific Ocean* 23d March, 1806, where they arrived in November, 1805;—and where some American vessels had been just before.—They state the Indians to be as numerous on the *Columbia* river, which empties into the *Pacific*, as the whites in any part of the U.S. They brought a family of the *Mandan* indians with them. The winter was very mild on the *Pacific.*—They have kept an ample journal of their tour; which will be published, and must afford much intelligence.

While in Washington, D.C., Lewis made sure that his men were given land and money as a reward for going on the expedition. He also worked on the notes that he had made during the trip. The president wanted Lewis to **publish** the journals so that everyone could read about his adventures. However, Lewis never finished them.

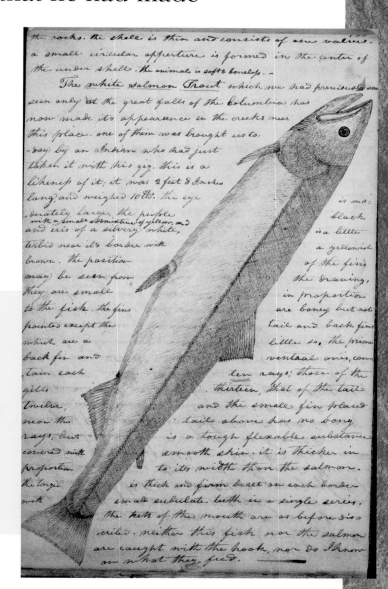

President Jefferson had asked Lewis to take careful notes of everything he saw during the journey. This picture in Lewis's journal is of a white salmon trout.

Life After the Expedition

In 1807, President Jefferson appointed Lewis **governor** of the Louisiana **Territory.** Before he left Washington, D.C., Lewis wrote a paper about the fur trade. He also traveled to Virginia where he hoped to find a wife. He met many young women, but he never married.

Lewis's Firsts

Lewis was the first American explorer to:

- *describe or draw over 100 kinds of birds and animals*
- *describe or draw over 200 kinds of plants*
- *meet and describe over 50 groups of Native American peoples*

In the late 1800s, St. Louis was a leading transportation and trade center because of its location on the Missouri and Mississippi Rivers.

The watch that Lewis took with him on the **expedition** can be seen at the Missouri Historical Society Museum in St. Louis.

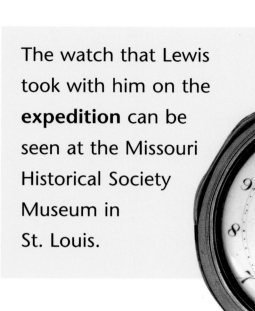

Lewis tried to be a good governor, but he missed exploring. He worked with Native American chiefs to bring about peace. He met with important people, built roads, and began projects to make the territory a better place.

He moved alone to St. Louis in 1808. When Lewis heard that William Clark and his wife were moving to St. Louis, he found them a home. Lewis ate many meals with the Clarks. When the Clarks had a baby boy, they named him Meriwether Lewis Clark in honor of their good friend.

Lewis's Last Days

Lewis saw a bright future for the Louisiana **Territory.** He bought land and went into business with a fur trading company. Lewis worked hard to keep the peace. It cost a lot of money to pay soldiers, buy supplies, and build **forts.** When he asked government officials in Washington, D.C., for money to pay some of the bills, they said no. Lewis was very upset. He decided to go to Washington, D.C., to speak with the new U.S. president, James Madison.

When Lewis and his team came upon the three forks of the Missouri River, Lewis named one of the rivers the Madison, in honor of President James Madison.

The Journals

Lewis's journals were published in 1814, several years after he died. The journals proved to the world that Lewis was a great American hero.

Lewis started out on the journey to Washington, D.C. He never made it there. He died of a gunshot wound on October 11, 1809, in Tennessee. He was only 35 years old.

Lewis's sudden death saddened many people, especially William Clark and Thomas Jefferson, the people who knew him best. Meriwether Lewis had been a strong leader who loved his country and faced danger bravely.

Lewis is buried at Meriwether Lewis Park in Hohenwald, Tennessee.

Glossary

astronomy study of the stars

botany study of plants

Congress part of U.S. government that makes the laws

declare say clearly or announce

estate fine country house on a large piece of land

expedition journey taken for a special purpose

fort strong building used for defense against enemy attack

geography study of places

governor person who is in charge of a state or territory

herb plant used as medicine

interpreter person who explains what someone is saying in another language

Louisiana Purchase western half of the Mississippi River basin purchased in 1803 from France by the United States

malaria disease that causes chills and fevers

Nez Percé member of a Native American people of Idaho, Washington, and Oregon

plantation large estate with many workers

private person of low rank in the military

promote give a more important job

publish make into a book for readers

Revolutionary War war from 1775 to 1783 in which the American colonists won freedom from Great Britain

survey measure and map land

territory part of the United States that is not yet a state

Whiskey Rebellion uprising against taxes on liquor

More Books to Read

DeVillier, Christy. *Lewis & Clark*. Edina, Minn.: ABDO, 2001.

Herbert, Janis. *Lewis and Clark for Kids*. Chicago: Chicago Review Press, 2000.

Isaacs, Sally Senzell. *America in the Time of Lewis and Clark*. Chicago: Heinemann Library, 1999.

Johmann, Carol A. *The Lewis and Clark Expedition*. Charlotte, Vt.: Williamson Publishing, 2002.

Patent, Dorothy Hinshaw. *Animals on the Trail with Lewis and Clark*. New York: Clarion, 2002.

Places to Visit

Fort Clatsop National Memorial (reconstructed fort)
92343 Fort Clatsop Road
Astoria, Oregon 97103
Visitor Information: (503) 861-2471

Jefferson National Expansion Memorial
11 North 4th Street
St. Louis, Missouri 63102
Visitor Information: (314) 655-1700

The North Dakota Lewis & Clark Interpretive Center
P.O. Box 607
Washburn, ND 58577-0607
Visitor Information: (701) 462-8535

Index